The Industrial Institute for Economic and Social Research

The Political Economy of the Welfare State

by James Buchanan

Distribution: Almqvist & Wiksell International, Stockholm, Sweden
© James Buchanan and The Industrial Institute for Economic and Social
Research.
ISBN 91-7204-296-6
Cover design: Stefan Lehtilä Tecknare AB
gotab Stockholm 1988 87205

The Political Economy of the Welfare State

Preface

Professor James Buchanan received the Prize in Economic Science in Memory of Alfred Nobel in 1986. As part of the established tradition IUI and the Federation of Swedish Industries invited him back to Sweden to give a lecture on a topic of his choice.

We are happy to publish the lecture presented at the IUI on August 28, 1987. The *"Political Economy of the Welfare State"* is the topical theme for a number of industrial nations, but perhaps most particularly so for Sweden.

Stockholm in May 1988

Gunnar Eliasson

The Socialist State and the Transfer State

Let me commence with some basic definitions. I shall make a clear distinction between the "socialist state" and the "transfer state". In the first, the state, through its various arms and agencies, directly provides goods and services, whether these be "public" (or collective consumption) goods and services, in some meaningfully defined technological sense, or "private" (partitionable) goods. That is to say, the "socialist state" is a direct producer; it accords with the Marxist norm of controlling the means of production. By contrast, at least as an ideal type, the "transfer state" does not directly provide goods and services, nor does it directly finance such goods and services. The "transfer state", as an ideal type, simply takes tax funds from some individuals and groups in its jurisdiction and transfers these funds, in the form of cash payments, to other individuals and groups in the political community.

The Welfare State and the Churning State

What I shall refer to as the "welfare state" is a form of the transfer state. It is to be distinguished from another possible form of the transfer state, which I shall call the "churning state", to take a term from Anthony de Jasay's book, *The State* (1985). The "churning state" simply takes tax payments from some groups and offers cash payments to other groups depending on the relative political power of the competing coalitions as they interact through the political decision process. There need be no connection at all between the net pattern of the transfers that take place and any agreed-upon norms for advancing the welfare or well-being of members of the community. There need be, in particular, no shift in the final distribution of incomes toward those least favored. Quite the opposite may happen. The pattern of transfers in the churning state is exclusively determined by the struggle among competing interests through the political process, whatever this may be, and there need be no connection with redistribution, as normatively interpreted. George Stigler has referred to the churning state as operating in accordance with what he calls the Director's law of redistribution.

The "welfare state", again as an ideal type, is to be contrasted with the "churning state" precisely in the sense that it does operate to further or to promote well-defined norms of welfare, norms that have traditionally been considered meaningful objectives, at least for many members of the community. The transfers that take place within the welfare state embody a systematic pattern or patterns. Tax payments are exacted from some persons and groups, and cash transfers are made to other persons and groups, but these are redistributional in a broadly defined and normatively evaluated sense. There is some quasi-legitimate purpose involved other than the mere interplay of special interests seeking political favors in the form of cash payments. The major programs of the welfare state are familiar to us all. These programs involve taxation of the general public through either direct or indirect taxation with the revenues utilized to make payments to the elderly in the form of social security or retirement pensions, to the poor in the form of means-tested grants, to children in the form of family allowances, to the sick, to the disabled, to the handicapped, to other groups that qualify in particular features of their existence.

These groups may be politically organized, and they usually are, along with the bureaucratic agencies that are built up to support continuation and expansion of these payments, but they are to be distinguished from the recipient groups in the churning state, whose very existence depends on the potential for qualifying for transfers. The churning state makes transfers to farmers or agricultural interests, to protected producers of import substitutes, to college and university students and aca-

8

demic faculties, to consumers of municipal transport services, to airline passengers, to government workers, to various and sundry other groups that cannot qualify for inclusion under any meaningfully defined "welfare state" rubric.

It is clear from this comparative listing here that, in almost any modern state, the welfare state and the churning state are intermingled, and that the tendency is for any pure welfare state to move in the direction of the churning state. But it remains nonetheless useful to make the distinction between these two forms of the transfer state. The difference between these two forms lies in the existence of a quasi-legitimate basis for the welfare state, for that set of fiscal transfers, taxes and cash payments, that describe its operation.

The classification of observed and existing transfer programs into the two sets is not an easy task, and especially when we recognize that all transfer programs will be proposed and defended in terms of the fulfillment of some general public purpose. And economists can always be found who will provide what seems to be plausibly acceptable arguments. Even the most blatant "pork barrel" programs, exemplified in my own country by the Tulsa and Tombigbee canals, are discussed in the language of furthering the "public interest". Descriptive accuracy in the full sense would presumably require that transfer programs be arrayed along a continuum, from those that clearly embody normatively acceptable welfare-enhancing redistributional results to those that generate welfare-reducing redistributional rules with little or no offsetting generalizable public benefits. I suggest that it remains nonetheless useful to impose the two-part classification suggested, so long as we keep in mind that the discussion proceeds in terms of ideal types.

The Legitimacy of the Welfare State

I suggested above that the distinction between the two types of transfer state is located in the quasi-legitimacy of the welfare state.

By quasi-legitimacy, I mean that it is possible to advance a justificatory argument in support of the institutions of the welfare state, at least in the abstract, and independently of any prior consideration of implementation, that is of the prospects for practical operation of any such set of transfers. How is this justification derived?

I think that the contractarian model is the appropriate one here, and I have long associated myself with what I call a constitutional contractarian position. That is to say, an institution is legitimized or justified, at least conceptually, if we can think of that institution as having been approved, in principle, on some agreement in a hypothetical contract in which all persons participate but when no person is able fully to identify his or her own role or position under the operation of the institution so approved. The contractarian device here is that of the veil of ignorance and/or uncertainty in which the individual contractor is forced to choose as if he or she does not know who he or she will be and hence how the workings of an institution will affect personal positions. This device has been made widely familiar to social philosophers by John Rawls who used the veil of ignorance in deriving principles of justice in his 1971 book, *A Theory of Justice*. The device was introduced much earlier, as a veil of uncertainty, by Gordon Tullock and me when we wrote *The Calculus of Consent* (1962).

The point here is that, with some such construction, we can justify basic constitutional authorization for a set of institutions that will implement transfers designed to further the redistributional norms associated with the welfare state. As presented in *The Calculus of Consent,* the individual, if he or she is uncertain as to where his or her personal economic position will be, may agree to set up an institution that will provide insurance against location in worst-case distributional positions. There may be agreement on a set of safety-net transfers that will insure against falling into the depths of poverty, against losing abilities to earn income productively, against medical disasters, etc. It should be noted, however, that any such justificatory argument must leave the precise details open-ended, so to speak. The procedural requirements of hypothetical contract do not allow for precise descriptions of these institutions. (In this respect, I differ sharply with John Rawls, who attempted, in my view, to be much too precise in defining just what "principles" would emerge from the idealized contract.)

The other side of the point here is that *no* such justification can be mounted for the transfers of the churning state. It is simply not possible to derive even a hypothetical agreement at the ultimate constitutional level on institutions that would implement transfers to particular consumers or producers of designated product or product groups in the economy, that would specifically inhibit freedom of economic exchange in order to further the purely distributional interests of designated groups who happen to hold differentially higher political power in the decision structure.

So much for the philosophical justification of some of the institutions that we associate with the term "welfare state" and with the absence of comparable philosophical justification for the institutions of fiscal transfer that we associate with the "churning state". It should be evident from the discussion that the dividing line between these two pure forms is difficult to maintain or even to discern in practice, and, further, that any constitutional authorization of the institutions of the welfare state tends, at the same time, to open the doors of political manipulation later; but first, I want to discuss problems of implementation of the welfare state, unsullied by any shift toward the churning state.

The Politics of the Transfer State

Let me indicate some of the difficulties here by telling you an autobiographical story. Geoffrey Brennan and I published a book, *The Power to Tax*, in 1980. In this exercise, we asked the question: How much taxing authority would the individual behind the appropriate veil of ignorance or uncertainty grant to the government? We derived, so to speak, the structure of a tax constitution. But, as we stated explicitly, the whole exercise was specifically restricted to the government that provided or financed goods and services, public goods as normally described, and without authorization to make fiscal transfers. Our plan was to follow up that book with a companion sequel, which we were to call *The Power to Transfer,* and in which we hoped to derive principles for constitutional agreement on those institutions of the welfare state previously discussed. Needless to say, this second book has not been written. It has proved to be extraordinarily hard to develop any acceptable analytical framework here. The reason lies in deriving and utilizing any model of how ordinary politics work in the making of fiscal transfers that will not quickly degenerate into the churning state. That is to say, the philosophical argument is easy; the political argument is almost impossible. Or to put the point somewhat differently, if we include problems of political implementation in the argument, it may be impossible to mount a satisfactory justification of the institutions of the welfare state.

Let me give you a hint of what is at issue here through a simple example. Suppose that, behind a veil of ignorance about who we are to be, that is, just where we are to be individually located in the income distribution, pre-tax, pre-transfer, we should all agree that those persons who happen to end up in the lower decile of the distribution may be supported by cash transfers paid by taxes levied on those in the upper ninety per cent of the distribution. Well and good. Or, if you prefer, we could state the setting differently and say that persons who earn no income or, say, less than one fifth of the median income, may be supported from tax monies levied on the others in the community. Suppose that one or more of these schemes is constitutionally authorized; the government is empowered to tax for the purpose of making such transfers.

But what government will have much incentive to carry out any such constitutional mandate? Those persons who are in the lowest decile of the income distribution in any period will not have much political clout; no government will find it advantageous to favor this group differentially. Political support must be more broadly based. Government will, however, have a very strong incentive to use the authorization to transfer so as to gain political support. The incentive will be to widen or to broaden the range of those who might be eligible for cash payments and to reduce those who are within the scope of taxation for funding the transfers. The government, no matter how organized, will have an incentive to expand the eligibility to receive cash payments from the lowest decile to, say, the lowest three or four deciles, or, in the limit, to the lowest fifty per cent of the electorate. There is a natural proclivity on the part of political leaders to want to expand the range of eligibility for receipt of transfers, no matter how the program is initially authorized. The same pressures exist for the taxing side of the ledger; there will be a natural tendency for political leaders to reduce the size of the group that is subjected to net tax payments. There will emerge some sort of political equilibrium here, but it may bear little or no relationship to the sort of welfare state that might have been initially authorized at some basic constitutional level.

The Over-Extension of the Welfare State

We can, I think, reach a conclusion about the consequences of the welfare state that is irrefutable, either in theory or in practice. The conclusion is that, in operation, any institution that is philosophically justified at some ultimate constitutional level, will be *overextended* beyond any limits of constitutional justification. That is to say, the welfare state, in practice, will always be larger and more inclusive than the welfare state in principle. And from this conclusion, it follows that the overextension in practice may well be, although not necessarily, such as to destroy the justification in the first place. This result cannot be generalized; but it does suggest that any examination of the justification of an institution of the welfare state must reckon on the costs of the possible overextension. This cost will emerge as a necessary part of the political structure almost independently of how the political decision process is organized, regardless of how close this process might approach that of idealized majoritarian democracy, whatever this might be.

This conclusion about overextension as a necessary consequence of the welfare state suggests that reform movement aimed simply at bringing the welfare programs within plausibly defined grounds of initial constitutional intent and justification may be doomed to failure. The overextension is a natural outgrowth of the institutions of fiscal transfers operating within a political structure that is responsive to constituency pressures, which includes almost all political structures. This conclusion also suggests that the critical step lies in the initial constitutional authorization for the implementation of welfare state transfers.

An initial constitutional authorization could, of course, specify the limits of application of transfers justified under normatively acceptable redistributional arguments. The existence of such limits would seem to eliminate the prospect for overextension that I have emphasized. The problem here is one of incentive compatibility. The institutions of majoritarian democracy are unlikely to respect constitutionally authorized limits if these limits are directly counter to the incentives of political agents. Constitutionally authorized, or otherwise legitimized, transfer programs must be implemented through the institutions of ordinary politics. It seem unrealistic to expect that compliance with constitutional limits on extension and application of transfer programs will emerge, even if these limits are quite specifically laid down.

Most modern states are well beyond any initial constitutional authorization. Welfare states exist, along with churning states, and the institutions of these two states are descriptive of most if not all modern nations. What are some other consequences of these institutions, as they are observed to operate? The fact that they are overextended beyond all limits of legitimacy may be acknowledged. But what other consequences do these overextended institutions produce?

Note, first of all, that the overextension discussed above will take place independently of any incentive effects of the institutions of welfare transfer. Even if there are no "economic" consequences of the familiar sort, we should get the overextension as a result of the proclivity of the political decision makers to respond positively to the desires of constituents.

The Economics of Welfare Transfers: Rent Seeking

But, of course, these more familiar incentives will exist and they will have predictable consequences. These consequences are of several varieties. Let me first discuss a consequence that is related to but different from that which produces the overextension already discussed. This overextension, as presented, stems from the natural proclivities of politicians in office who try to respond to constituency demands. But this overextension is aided and abetted by the activity of aspiring politicians and of aspiring leaders of groups of potential recipients of transfers, who now have an incentive to initiate efforts to get their clients under the transfer umbrella, to get new and additional groups included under expanded eligibility requirements. In modern public choice theory, this activity takes the form that is called *rent seeking*. And the observation that transfer payments are being made by the state necessarily sets up incentives for those who seek to secure these payments, these "rents", to invest time and economic resources in those activities that will secure them. If the source of rents or profits is observed to lie within the political sector, as opposed to the market sector, we can surely predict that rent seekers or profit seekers will invest resources in an effort to secure these rents or profits. What the modern rent seeking theory emphasizes is, however, that when the attraction is governmental or state transfers, much of the rent seeking activity may amount, in the net, to pure resource wastage. Time and effort spent, for example, in trying to convince politicians to expand this or that program may, in the net, be socially wasteful, since there will be competing attempts to secure what must be, ultimately, scarce resources. In my own country, we have observed that during the last three decades, more and more lobbying groups have organized and set up headquarters in the Washington ares. These establishments hire many lawyers, economists, consultants, and others for the sole purpose of influencing politicians to expand program benefits to their constituents. Such effort, or investment, is clearly productive for the successful group that gets the governmental handouts. But these efforts are likely to be socially wasteful; there is no net contribution to valued product, which these resources could have made in the absence of such efforts.

As I have previously noted, the line between the programs of the welfare state and the churning state becomes difficult to draw in any case, and this is particularly the case with these efforts to influence the direction and size of transfers. Since rents or profits are perceived to originate from the governmental sector, from the state, there is likely to be investment made in attempts to secure potential rents over and beyond those that may or may not have been constitutionally authorized or which may have had some semblance of constitutional-philosophical legitimacy. Sitting politicians, for example United States congressmen, are not likely to make much distinction between the protectionist pressure from the steel or the automobile industries and the welfare state pressures from

16

the elderly, the disabled, or the ill, along with the supporting industries and bureaucracies.

To summarize my argument to this point I have suggested two important consequences of the welfare state, the *over-extension* of transfers (and supporting taxes) beyond any philosophically justified limits and the potential *wastage* of valued economic resources in efforts to secure and to extend such transfers.

The Economics of Welfare Transfers: Excess Burdens

I have not, to this point, discussed the more familiar economic incentives that arise from the welfare state program of transfers and taxes directly. These familiar excess-burden effects would be the first that come to mind to economists. The program of welfare transfers must, themselves, affect both those who are subjected to the taxes required to finance the payments and those who receive the payments. I need not go into the simple analytics of excess burden analysis. Any tax that is levied on the receipt of income, at the margin of adjustment between earning and not-earning income, will reduce the amount of effort expended and will, in the process, generate an excess-burden, a welfare loss that is not recouped by those who secure the receipts. This welfare loss is, of course, dependent in magnitude on the level of marginal tax rates. The effects on the side of potential transfer recipients are the obverse of those on the side of taxpayers. Those who receive cash transfers have less incentive to work to earn income, and particularly so as and if the eligibility for transfers is reduced as income is earned. Many modern welfare state programs, at least those with which I am familiar in my own country, embody highly perverse incentive structures in the receipts side of the transfers. Recipients are actively discouraged from earning income.

In a somewhat more elementary sense, economic theory tells us that demand for anything will increase as the price falls. From this elementary lesson in economics, we can predict that if the price of obtaining income falls, we can expect more and more demanders for such income to arise. It is little surprise then to learn that as we, in the United States, have sought to make more and more funds available for cash transfers, the potential demanders of such transfers have increased and increased dramatically over the period of the modern welfare state, and particularly over the period since the so-called Great Society of the 1960's which was established under the guidance of President Johnson. In a widely heralded book, published in 1985, *Losing Ground,* Charles Murray was successful in documenting the increase in the demands on the welfare state that the very existence of this state has created. There is much discussion in my country now about how the separate programs of this modern welfare state have created and are creating a permanent subclass of welfare recipients, who do not know what work is and who are now multi-generational in their welfare recipient roles.

Prospects for Reform

All of the consequences of the welfare state reduce the productive potential of a national economy, while at the same time the programs of the welfare state fall short of achieving any of the objective norms for which they were initially established. On this, there is near universal agreement among modern economists who have looked at these programs in almost any country. But having said this, having advanced this as diagnosis, it becomes then much more difficult to point forward any effective reform. It is not at all easy to dismantle the welfare state, even when the overextensions beyond all legitimate range are fully acknowledged.

There are several barriers to effective reform. First of all, persons have established expectations about potential continued eligibility for transfers. These expectations cannot be thwarted without political repercussions that modern politicians cannot accept. As an example, in the United States of the 1980's, the entitlements under the old-age or social security system cannot even so much as be discussed politically, and this despite general acknowledgement of budgetary stringency. This welfare program is politically sacrosanct, beyond the boundaries of political discourse, and it is considered political suicide if a politician breaks this rule. Even modest attempts at reform are very quickly countered. In 1981, there was a modest attempt to raise the age for early retirement, a fully rational adjustment given the change in longevity. But this was quickly shut off, to the political cost of those who proposed the change. Even the Congress itself recognized the abuses under the disability part of the system, and made an effort to tighten up eligibility requirements. This was met with such a resounding rejection by political recipients that Congress reversed its own policy a mere two years after its initiation.

In the United States we did, perhaps surprisingly, succeed in eliminating the mistaken double indexing of program benefits under the retirement system in 1982. And there has been a moratorium on new programs of the welfare state for about a decade. Even this aspect may be changing in 1988, as we are now discussing a new program for catastrophic illness. We have, for about a decade, been in an equilibrium of sorts, with few new initiatives, but with little or no cutting back on programs already in existence. I fear the upsurge of demands for new programs if and when the political leadership of our country changes.

The Welfare State Mentality

But over the longer term, I fear the implications of the welfare state mentality that has developed among the citizenry, not only in my country, but in yours and in most other modern states. I fear what seems to be a loss of the old fashioned work ethic, which now seems to motivate the Japanese, the Korean, the Taiwanese, but not the citizenry of either North or South America. Or that of Europe. I have recently been working on the work ethic, and I come to the view that this ethic is properly named. There must be an ethic of work, or effort, and there is economic content in this ethic that economists have not been able to incorporate in their sometimes fancy theories. This ethic must be restored or at the very least maintained and strengthened, if we are to maintain prosperity, peace, and civil order. The demise of this work ethic is partially due to the overextension and continuation of the welfare state. We cannot, and perhaps should not, dismantle this state in any total sense. But we can trim its edges, we can stop the bleeding, and above all, we can work at restoring that sense of basic values that deems productive effort in the marketplace as "good" and that scorns the receipt of governmental handouts as socially unworthy. The challenge is really not with the economists among us; the economic consequences are well recognized. And the political economy which makes reform so difficult and overextension so easy is also coming to be a part of the conventional wisdom of the social sciences. I suggest that the challenge lies with those who must promulgate and instill and transmit the "civic religion" of traditional classical liberalism, in which the self-reliant individual remains jealous of his own liberty and confident in his own ability to secure his own welfare under the legal umbrella of a constitutionally constrained state.

DISCUSSION

Gunnar
Eliasson

In many countries an increasing share of the population has become dependent on the public sector in various ways, both through income transfers and through employment in the public sector. By now the majority of the Swedish population is dependent on the public sector in this way. How would you look at that?

James
Buchanan

Obviously, it makes it much more difficult to get any kind of effective reform as more people get dependent on the public sector. You get a clear conflict of interest. I would never suggest that getting reform is easy. It is hard to motivate people to look beyond their self interest. Things may need to get much worse before they get much better. It seems we must understand that people have expectations that have been built up for continuation of program benefits under the welfare state. I do not think any political party or government can propose changes that would simply violate those expectations. I think you have to meet those expectations to the extent that it is possible. You can work out schemes by imaginative design so you can meet those expectations, while at the same time change the programs so they will not build up such expectations. In my paper on dismantling the welfare state I proposed a scheme which involved a massive buyout, in which you compensate people for the capital value of their expectations of what they have built up under the system but then you change the system from this point on such that people will in fact be operating under a more viable system.

Richard Murray	The last part of the lecture reminded me of a book written by Bertrand Russel. I wonder if you are familiar with it. The title is very telling. It is "In Praise of Idleness".
James Buchanan	No, I don't know that book but I will look at it. What is his thesis?
Richard Murray	His thesis is that much of the evil in the world is created by too much work rather than too little.
James Buchanan	Well, I take the position just categorically opposite to that. Imagine yourself the following: You are in a spaceship and you may or may not like to work. It doesn't matter. You can land in either of two countries. These countries are identical in all respects, in resources, in the number of people, the type of people and everything. It is just that in one of the countries people work two times as much as in the other. You can land your spaceship in either country and become a citizen in that country. You can work as much as you want. There is nothing compulsory. If you don't want to work hard you don't have to. In which country do you want to land your spaceship? It seems obvious that you land your space ship in the country where they work the hardest, because you get more of the surplus generated by a more productive economy. Since there will be more goods available, you would be better off in the country where everybody work hard.
Curt Nicolin	I want to take issue with your example. If I was in a spaceship and I had the option of landing in China or in the U.S., I would land in the U.S. (disregarding all political aspects). The reason is that even if I only worked half as much in the

U.S. I would still enjoy a much higher living standard there than I would in China. The important thing is the base of knowledge and investment that has been made in the past. That's much more important than how many hours you work. If I liked to work very hard, I would make an entirely different choice.

A different point: If a politician says to his voters that he wants to reduce welfare expenditures and taxes, he would have a very slim chance of being elected. But if he goes to them and says that I'm going to offer you something that's more than an extended welfare state, then he would win, if he has the right program. What it is that is worth more than more public welfare is an open question. But if the politician cannot offer us something that is better than a marginal improvement in the welfare state, then he can attack your churning state.

James Buchanan	I have no comment or objection to your last point. On your first point the economists couldn't get by without the word ceteris paribus and in my example I specified that other things equal; the same technology, the same population, the same basic resources. That was a constructed example, that your example didn't contradict at all.
Erik Fredborg	The word churn is exactly the same word as the Swedish word "kärna". It stems from the same root.

A question: Is it not inevitable that governments very soon find themselves living beyond their resources and consequently turn to inflation? And is, as a consequence of this, inflation not a predominantly political problem?

James Buchanan	I think that is right. As I was arguing earlier, you tend to get this overextension as a result of pushing political forces and this overextension leads to heavy taxation, which, in turn, leads you to use indirect or hidden forms of taxation such as inflation or big deficits. Yes, the whole thing is a political problem. You get a breakdown in the structure, when the welfare state exceeds certain limits. So the real question is, in a dynamic setting, is there a meaningful equilibrium that can be reached or does it just go on until you get a breakdown? There is a bit of evidence, it seems to me, in the last two or three decades that we may have reached a limit and some equilibrium. You wouldn't predict that in the next three decades the public sector will expand in any country. It's even likely that there will be some minor cutbacks. There are discussions about reducing the scope of government intrusion, about privatization in the socialist state–which, of course, I didn't talk about. If you make a prediction, you would say that the public sector will be marginally reduced in the future. Not dramatically reduced, but certainly not dramatically expanded.
Clas Wihlborg	You talked about the need for some constitutional rule, in a sense of distributing welfare payments in a contractual kind of framework. It is assumed that one could agree on such a thing "behind the veil of ignorance", and in a constitutional setting establish it. Now, would Hayek's suggested constitutional rule solve the problem of the welfare state? His outline for constitution allows for a supreme court, with more power than the U.S. supreme court, which could check the constitutionality of what the government does. Would that kind of system in some way be

able to deal with the political mechanism of ever increasing welfare expenditures?

James Buchanan

It might. Hayek's constitutional proposals were more geared toward a parliamentary kind of government, which he proposed would have a second upper level house which would, in a sense, be a constitutional court acting to constrain the lower house. The ordinary parliamentary, majoritarian system, no doubt, could be designed in such a way that it might be able to implement something like what we're thinking about. You see, what we want to prevent is simply shifting majority coalitions from agreeing to expand and carry forward these programs, always to benefit the particular majority behind the particular coalition that was pushing at the time. If you had agreed on some sort of basic fundamental institutions of transfer, then no doubt, a Hayek kind of scheme could, in fact, do something about enforcing that. I haven't thought about that in detail.

Ingemar Ståhl

In making the distinction between the welfare state and the "churning state" it is interesting to consider some of the empirical magnitudes behind it. We have made some calculations on Swedish data. The starting point is that public sector spending is roughly 65 per cent of GDP. Pure public goods, i.e., the functions of the Night Watchman state, are roughly 6-7 per cent of GDP in Sweden today. Adding to this what we might call the "infrastructure state", e.g., roads, bridges, and (possibly) the telephone service, we will get another 3-5 per cent. On top of this we have the "social state", which comprises risk and life-cycle insurance (health, unemployment,

25

pensions) and makes up another 25-35 per cent. Most of it can, in principle, be privately financed and produced. The redistribution to the really poor, those with handicaps that cannot be insured, is only 5 per cent. That leaves the "churning state" or the "interest group state", which accounts for the remaining 20-30 per cent. The "legitimate" part of the welfare state would be very small indeed, if that which *could* be left in the private sector is left out of the public sector. For example, if we could switch from a tax financed pay-as-you-go system to a private fully funded system, the welfare state would boil down to about 15 per cent. And most of the rest is health care, which in most cases is pure insurance.

James Buchanan
I think these breakdowns are very interesting. I'm not sure I have seen any compatible attempts in the United States. Our total is less, about 40 per cent as opposed to your 65. I suspect our breakdown would be roughly equivalent within that lower limit and I think that's very interesting. Of course, you've got a problem; as you say, the major share of the welfare state part is due to your pension system. That would be true in our case, too. But it's not as if you could shift to a private system without a major buyout provision, because we have, in fact, a pay-as-you-go system and it has not been funded. It should have been funded, but it has not been funded.

Hans Werthén
There are two aspects of the welfare state in this country. One is the question of how much and what tax financed welfare, pensions, health care, etc., one should have. The other is how it is to be produced. In the last decades the tendency has

been to have increased government monopoly provision.

In the old times, of course, the class barriers in society were between have and have nots. Today it is a vertical line between those who are sitting snugly in local government monopolies and those who are exposed to competition in the private sector. The productivity difference between the two groups can be one to two very often. I don't expect opera singers to sing 10 per cent faster every year. But there are a lot of activities where you can improve productivity. Studies show that productivity in the Swedish public sector has fallen by about 1.5 per cent per year during the last 10 years. The incentive to do anything about it is nil. I see that as the biggest problem in this country. No party dares to do much about it, because they lose the votes of all these public sector employees. But also in this slow moving country there is now a slow reaction called "privatizing".

James Buchanan Certainly, I accept the point. It's something I haven't dealt with, but the delivery system have incentive effects. That's a very important part of the whole operation. To the extent that you can introduce, even if you don't privatize, competitive structures to some extent in your publicly operated systems you will, in fact, expect to have more efficiency. There is some discussion in my country and also in Britain about the possibility of changing the basic monopoly of the public school system. It has not got very far, but at least there is a discussion.

Birgitta Swedenborg I'm not sure that I have a question that has not already been asked. But are we to conclude from what you have said that the choice we face is between no transfer state at all, and one which is, in principle, unbounded or reaches an equilibrium at some very high expenditure level? That is, that no constitutional rule could keep the welfare state within the constitutionally agreed limit?

James Buchanan

Well, I'm not too happy about that implication. But some of my arguments will, in fact, lead to that implication. Once you start down that road, unless you will go to that high level equilibrium, the very function of your structure may be such that that's where you're led to. Now, let's get back to the point I made about the need to spend some time trying to invent designs for constitutional structures that will, in fact, put those equilibrium limits at lower levels, while at the same time accomplishing what we can legitimately justify at the constitutional level for these types of genuine welfare state objectives that we would all agree to. Maybe we would have to go back to some kind of change in our political decision rules. Maybe we would have to get away from the notion that always majority coalitions would be decisive. Maybe we ought to get back to the Wicksellian principle, where it has to be a 2/3 majority, or something like that, in order to approve extension of eligibility requirements or extensions of benefits. Then, perhaps, we can put procedural constraints on this kind of natural proclivity to expansion. But we need a lot of work on designing constitutional reforms.

Nils Carlsson

I'd like to question the first part of your thesis, namely, that it is possible to philosophically justify the welfare state. It is a very popular view in

Sweden. People would say that the welfare state is just. It seems to me that if you argue from a contractarian constitutional perspective it is impossible to justify the welfare state. In a contractarian perspective you would take into account how the system would work in reality, what incentives politicians have, what incentives voters have. Then, it would not be possible to justify the welfare state, since it deteriorates into the churning state. In addition, there is von Hayek's argument that social justice is meaningless, i.e., we can only talk about just rules and just procedures but we cannot talk about justice in outcomes or in some distributional sense. That would make it even harder to justify philosophically the welfare state.

James Buchanan	I think that's a very good point. It is a critical comment. There is no doubt that I may be vulnerable to that particular argument in the way I have stated the case here. It's certainly true that in some types of philosophical argument you cannot justify the welfare state. That is, if you take the natural right perspective that individuals have the rights to their own personal privacy, it is very difficult to come up with a philosophical justification. I was taking a contractarian position and the first point you raise is that you cannot justify the churning state kind of transfer, but you can justify the welfare state kind of transfer. At least, you can conceive of being behind the veil of ignorance trying to protect yourself against these consequences that somehow you want to protect against. I said, independently of taking any political implementation into account, you could come up with a justification. Now, if you take the political implementation

into account, realizing that you are going to have overextensions, realizing that you are going to have inefficiencies and difficulties to control the degeneracy of the system, I say it may immediately break down into a situation where you cannot justify it in the first place. I would accept that point. I may be vulnerable in the rethoric because of the way I presented the case in that paper. It may be that people will misinterpret that as a necessary philosophical justification for the institutions that exist. The point is that if you think of the political implementation, it may remove the philosophical justification that I started with – a kind of ideal world. It's a question of how I developed the rethoric. That's a really good point, I agree.

Gunnar Eliasson

The conclusion of your talk is that modern governments are not really taking responsibility for the long term. Rather they are myopic. And if everybody that is operating in the market are also myopic, as we know that we are, who is going to take care of the long term?

James Buchanan

Well, I think that opens up a whole set of possibilities and questions that I think is probably the most serious problem of all. Not only in terms of the transfers but also in terms of deficits and in terms of inflation. All these things reflect the absence of saving – in my own country anyway. They reflect a very high discount rate and nobody seems to take into account future levels of well being. I come more and more to the view that the Victorians really had it right. The Victorians knew they were not going to live always, but they acted as if they were going to live always and created institutions that they created for the purpose of being permanent institutions. I think we are all living on a capital value of that heritage. We have a much shorter time horizon in most aspects of our lives. How we can affect a shift back is a terrible problem. You can say there are many reasons for this. But correcting that is a part of the civic religion shift that I think we must go through, if we are going to preserve any resemblance whatsoever of the structure of civil order that we have in the western tradition.

Gunnar Eliasson   Shall we give Mr. Buchanan a big hand?